Ready to Eat the Sky

Kevin Pilkington

The River City Poetry Series
RIVER CITY PUBLISHING
Montgomery, Alabama

© 2004 by Kevin Pilkington.
All rights reserved under International and Pan-American Copyright Conventions. No part of this publication may be reproduced, stored in a retrieval system, or transmitted in any form or by any means electronic, or mechanical, through photocopying, recording, or otherwise, without the prior written permission of the publisher.

Published in the United States by River City Publishing
1719 Mulberry St.
Montgomery, AL 36106.

Designed by Lissa Monroe

First Edition—2004
Printed in the United States of America
1 3 5 7 9 10 8 6 4 2

Library of Congress Cataloging-in-Publication Data:

Pilkington, Kevin.
Ready to eat the sky / Kevin Pilkington.
p. cm. -- (The River City poetry series)
ISBN 1-57966-014-2
I. Title. II. Series.
PS3566.I51117R43 2004
813'.54--dc22
    2003021104

For Celia

"Just once before I die
 I want to climb up on a
 tenement sky
 to dream my lungs out …"

                                        Miguel Piñero

"The sky must and always shall with me be an effectual part of the composition."

                                        John Constable

Table of Contents

Acknowledgments

I. Shadow Boxing
  Turning Things Around 13
  If You Want to Drive Rather than Walk
      The Rest of the Way Home 15
  Where You Want to Be 17
  Martin Scorsese's Mother 19
  Birthday 21
  A Few Extra Days 23
  Getting By 25
  Street Music 28
  Going Fishing in Connecticut 31
  Shadow Boxing 33

II. Taxi Ride
  Breakfast for Free 37
  The Truth About Paris 39
  Learning to Pray 41
  Dogs 43
  Born Again 45

The Corner Where Jimmy Cagney Learned
 How to Act Tough 47
Apple Spider 50
Taxi Ride 52

III. The Amalfi Coast
First Day on the Amalfi Coast 57
Grilled Fish 59
Swimming 61
The Ride to Amalfi 63
The Last Saint 65
St. Andrew's Head 67

IV. Leaning Against August
Two Nickels 73
Flying South 76
Sand 79
Stems 81
Lungs 83
While You Are Away .86
Spine 87
Renting July 88
Kansas in My Lungs .90
Leaning Against August 92

Acknowledgments

Acknowledgment is made to the following periodicals in which these poems have appeared in various forms:

Columbia: Taxi Ride
Cortland Review: Two Nickels, Renting July
Evansville Review: Kansas in My Lungs
5 AM: Grilled Fish
Graffiti Rag: Born Again, Spine, The Truth About Paris
Greensboro Review: Where You Want to Be
Hayden's Ferry: The Last Saint
Inkwell: Lungs, First Day on the Amalfi Coast, Swimming, Apple Spider, While You Were Away
The Ledge: After Rain, Birthday, Leaning Against August
Louisville Review: If You Want to Drive Rather than Walk the Rest of the Way Home
Midland Review: Getting By
Rattle: St. Andrew's Head
Red Rock Review: Breakfast for Free, Going Fishing, A Few Extra Days
River Oak Review: Turning Things Around, Martin Scorsese's Mother
Turnstile: Learning to Pray

Some of the poems have appeared in the following chapbooks:
Reading Stone, Jeanne DuVal Editions
Getting By, The Ledge
St. Andrew's Head, Camber Press

I. Shadow Boxing

Turning Things Around

No matter how long a shower
I take, I still can't get this city
clean. I guess it doesn't matter
since I always knew I'd make it
to the top and now I have: fifth floor
of a five-flight walk-up. It's a place
where I can shine like that guy
did in math class back in high school.
For him it was grades, the right answers.
For me it's heat; with no a.c. I come up
with the right amount of sweat every
time. And I finally got the ringing
in my head to go away as soon
as I stopped paying the phone bill.
Within days I started getting in shape
after noticing how 1st Avenue with its heavy
traffic shed a few cars and is now
down to a single lane. So I started
running with it along the river too.
Have also been reading more but found
the quickest read was the face
of the woman on the 3rd floor
who always smiled as I walked
past her. She helped me quit
smoking when I found out nothing
could get me as high as her skirt.

And things keep getting better now
that I have a real identity. A couple
of months ago I wanted to know more
about my ancestors and started to trace
my family tree back to a maple in a park
across town then quit when I found
out I was Celtic. I discovered it
by accident during dessert, last Friday night
when the cake I ordered kept crumbling
onto the plate like an Irish castle.

If You Want to Drive Rather than Walk the Rest of the Way Home

When you are on the road
under a sky you don't understand
every time it talks crow, stay with it
until you reach a dead cat lying
in the grass; his eyes are yellow
from the headlights on the car
that hit him. Rain has already
turned his fur rust, his belly
is still white from years of rubbing
against snow and every breeze
that passes through his open mouth
rips on teeth.

Across from him are two roads.
Take the one he didn't reach—
it's thin and gravel and sounds
like an old man clearing his throat
if your feet drag. It runs through
fields that were once Indian burial
grounds, so don't worry if a pickup
truck passes you with a ghost
of dust behind it, since the soil
it usually carries is haunted
with bone.

Where the road curves there's
a farm house the color of drought,
reminding you even here things
can go wrong and that you are right
so keep going. A quarter mile on
there's an orchard that looks apple
but is peach and then a potato
field that adds starch to the air
and if you're not careful a few
inches around your lungs.

You'll then come to a meadow
where blades of grass are dull
enough for cows to graze and never
cut themselves. Look for a horse
who wears a hat of flies in case
it rains, feed him an apple
you should have taken from
the orchard and he'll take you down
a small ravine to an old truck.
It lost its paint and tires
a few wars ago, but climb in
behind the wheel, start it up
with your throat, then sit back
and drive home, listening
to all those weeds in its engine purr.

Where You Want to Be

You wake early again
get out of bed, walk over
to the window and look down
at the street to see if anything
has changed and, of course,
it never does.

At first you think the blanket
in the vacant lot near
the corner is new until
a gust of wind blows it
into the air and shreds
it into a flock of pigeons.

And if all the new clubs
make sure the city never
sleeps uptown the way the papers
claim, then the people under
cardboard in the alleys and in
front of doorways down here
every morning is how it finds
a way to nap.

The steeple on St. Bart's a few
blocks away is a spike that nails
Christ into the sky if you can't find
anything on the street to believe in

but it does nothing for the bent
trash cans standing along the curb
like arthritic old men who know
the real purpose of any life is found
in what everyone else throws away.

A woman coming out of the grocery
store on the corner of 4th in a short
skirt and heels does a better
job stopping traffic than
the red light hanging from
a wire that would rather swing
like Count Basie in strong
wind than stop every car
it should.

When you hear the woman
you admit you love start
breakfast, cracking an egg
open like the dawn, its yolk
a perfect tiny sun, you
are convinced this is where
you want to be, walking towards
her, hungry and ready
to eat the sky.

Martin Scorsese's Mother

The local into Grand Central
arrived late but shook the clock
on the train station wall back
ten minutes until it was on schedule
again. I took a seat in the last
car, opened up the *Times* in front
of me as if we were going to dance
then found an article on what went
wrong in my life but passed over it
since I never believe what I read.

I closed the paper gazed out
the window at the Bronx that looked
like an old friend who I turned
my back on years ago, and even
if I wanted could never patch
things up.

A guy in the seat across from me
facing Westchester asked if Fordham
was the next stop. He was in
a large brown sweat shirt
with the hood over his head
like a monk who didn't know Latin.

Before I could turn away
he wanted to know if the

movie director Martin Scorsese
still lived in the Bronx. It
was really Scorsese's mother
he wanted to meet, a little
white-haired woman the director
put in all his movies, more cameos
than major parts. He claimed she
stole every movie, an acting genius
who deserved an Oscar.

I wanted to sleep—told him
to find Arthur Avenue and start
knocking on doors until he
found hers. He smiled and thanked
me for the tip.

I looked out the window again
at a building on 116th. It was empty,
with broken windows like an old
woman who outlived her family.
I then rested my head against the seat,
closed my eyes and decided that tonight
I'd stay home, make dinner
and rent a movie, *Good Fellas* or maybe
even *Raging Bull*.

Birthday

You hitch into the city
and walk a few blocks
until you find a small
hotel you can afford.
If you didn't have to leave
the next day, you'd offer
to paint it since you need
the work—tell the owner
to buy enough for two coats
but brush the second onto
yourself because it's getting cold
and there's only a sweater
in your suitcase.

The manager behind the desk
has a cigar stuck in the side
of his mouth like a cork,
his bald head shining—
waxed the way the floor
needs to be. When you can't
remember your name, you pick
another just as good, sign in
then ask him if he knows
when the first bus leaves
in the morning. He says forget it
since the cheapest ride in town
is the next woman he can send

up to your room in fifteen minutes.

You take the elevator
to the fourth floor, open the door
to 407, check out the bed,
chair and sink before flipping
on the switch. A bulb hanging
from a wire lights up
like an idea you're glad
even you never had.

Throwing your suitcase on
the bed, you walk over
to look out the window.
An apartment light two blocks over
goes on and lights the top
of a water tower shaped like a candle
on the warehouse across the street.
It reminds you today
is your birthday and when
a switch or wind blows
the apartment light out
you close your eyes and make
a wish.

A Few Extra Days

On the beach years of wind
have finished carving rock
into the face of a beautiful
woman who stares out to sea,
her eyes soft and peasant,
towards Spain or wherever
waves translate into Spanish.
I make sure to wear my watch
whenever I stroll by since
she never gives me the time
of day. Even so I can't help
complimenting her stone.

The sun is intelligent down
here, not just bright—it knows
how to keep people like me
content, showing why the blues
can only mean water and sky
and never a job I lost or the last
woman who walked away.

Along this stretch of beach
and beyond the point with the palm
tree that looks like Bob Marley,
sailboats are knives sharpening
their blades on wind and the one
a few yards offshore looks out

of shape with its spinnaker a large
belly that must be full of beer
rather than wind hanging over its bow.

I've decided to stay a few extra
days and go sailing myself again.
Last night I left the harbor
at sunset, the sky the color
of a thin gold bracelet on the wrist
of a young girl. By midnight
I was lost until I used stars
lovers on land wouldn't need
to chart my way towards a bear
tamed by the moon then relaxed
and sailed towards the coast
under its paws.

Getting By

This old fishing village
is where the world turns
slowly on the blades
of a ceiling fan in a tavern
near the docks. I can
sit at the bar all day alone
and say nothing, dressed
in my favorite shirt—
the loud one that's quiet
enough for me to listen as locals
still talk tuna and drink extra
beer to add pounds on
the stories of whatever
they once caught.

I heard that before schools
were private and Protestant
in the next county, they
were a few miles offshore and bass.
Fisherman caught more waves
than needed, gutted them
for the fish inside, then threw
back any whitecaps
they couldn't use.

Things changed when most
fish were caught

and those that stayed
decided to keep their mouths shut.
Then the village tried but couldn't
catch tourists who went
for the beach a town up the coast
used for bait.

Even though I never grew
up around water and the only
fishing I ever did was for compliments,
the day I drove onto Main Street,
I could see this village had learned
to do what I've always done—
simply get by.

I saw it in the small shops
that were closed
and heavily salted with sea air
to keep them from spoiling in heat.

And later that night
how twilight over the harbor
was patched with stars
flags on boats lost in strong winds.
It was enough to make me stay.

Getting here is easy. Begin
with the last job you lose
or with a woman who believes
in you and says the moon

can be yours if you'll only reach for it.
Instead reach for another drink,
then sit back and do nothing
as the bourbon tells her that your old
car is big and yellow with a grill
grinning below a headlight
of eyes and is all the moon
you need.

The next day take 95 South
and keep driving until tired.
Turn on the local jazz station
and take the first exit between
Basie and Coltrane. Stay on that road.
It will pass through a piano
solo before leading into the village.

I'm beginning to think now
that I may never leave or even
bother looking for a real job.
What's the point when I know
every morning there will be a strong
breeze outside my window,
making leaves rustle like dollar
bills. It means I can afford
to stay in bed as long as I want,
since another day will come cheap.

Street Music

I'm on the street
where a guy once walked
up next to me and asked
for my wallet. I looked
at him then down at
the knife he was holding
and the point he was
trying to make. I
was convinced and handed
it over. The year before
crime had come down
with the old tenements
and new buildings went
up faster than rents.
I watched him run across
town with what was left
of the old neighborhood
in his coat pocket.

The entire area is safer
now but more expensive.
The shops along Third
were torn down. Most
came back as French
or Italian boutiques, some
never came back or
were lost in the translation.

Across the street the tallest
building yet is under
construction; at the end
of the day workers come down
covered in white dust
from rubbing against clouds.
It's going up on the spot
where the magazine store
stood. Its owner ran it
for sixty years and had
more stories in him than
the high-rise ever will.

Some things in the area
aren't what they seem.
Two years ago the section
of the river that runs
along the north side started
to jog and its banks
filled with concrete slabs
now closed on national holidays.
Although the traffic on First
is still heavy, cars
keep changing. What
stays the same and never
changes is the music
found in women walking
in heels that are so high
you need an elevator
just to reach their ankles.

Listen and you'll hear
their hips sway back
and forth with the kind
of songs you'll swallow
and never want to hum.

Going Fishing in Connecticut

I'm eight years old again,
my hair cut short
like lawns I pass
along Elm Street. No shirt
today to cover my thin chest
and ladder of ribs. Just
a donut of jeans rolled up
over my bare feet, and fishing
pole resting on my shoulder
like the rifle it becomes
as I begin marching, a soldier
going off to fun.

I turn right at the church
that shakes every Sunday
with hymns. God is Presbyterian
there until He is Methodist
in the church an hour later
in the next town. I walk
the dirt road that runs near
the cemetery, where Rebecca Osgood
is twelve forever, and the flowers
that grow from her knees every June.

I avoid stepping on rocks
that could hurt my feet
and wonder which ones are the kind

I heard my uncle say he wanted
his scotch poured on.
I make a left at the stone wall
a farmer built two hundred years ago
around his cows who became
trees after he died. A few maples
later, I reach the pond lying
on its back in a field.

Walking over to its edge,
I look down at my face
and watch a plane, gleaming
like a dime, fly into my right
ear. Before I can put my hand
over my left to block it from
leaving and add to my allowance,
it flies out. So I sit down
take the pole off my shoulder,
drop the line carefully into
the water, lie back and wait
for luck to bite.

Shadow Boxing

After his stroke
I wanted my father
the way he was:
picking up fifty-foot ladders
as if they were toys
and putting them on
his green truck that was
a bit darker than Dublin.

I didn't want his arm
hanging limp at his side.
Instead I wanted him
crouching over, throwing
a right cross at air,
a jab on the chin of a breeze,
finishing up with a flurry
and a blur of fists.
Then see that smile one more
time as he said, Not bad
for an old man of sixty-five.

On Monday I visited his grave
and no matter how green
the grass is, it never looks
like him.

When I left I wanted my father

back again, even if it meant
that last month when words
were tools he couldn't find,
or sitting on the edge
of his bed waiting for my mother
to dress him—his shoulders
thin and drooping.

II. Taxi Ride

Breakfast for Free

An article in the paper
you buy at the corner
newsstand says a murder
took place last night
just three blocks from where
you live. You almost called
the police with a lead
when you saw a woman
crossing the street ten
minutes ago in a short,
tight black dress with a body
that was a killer.

Heading home, you walk
past a building
where someone is playing
a classical piece on
the piano you've never
heard before, but it sounds
so sweet, it's the kind
of music you want to lick
rather than hear.

Near 2nd a guy comes
over and asks if you could
spare anything so he

could get something to eat.
After handing him the loose
change in your pocket,
you wish he were sober
so he could see how all
the cabs, stopping for the red
light, look like an omelette,
and how the hams hanging
in the butcher's window
along with the fresh
loaves of bread in the bakery
next to it make
the entire intersection
a great breakfast
that wouldn't even cost
him a dime.

The Truth About Paris

Most of my relationships
last as long as a drag
on a cigarette. This time
I gave up on Christ
then Buddha but now
pray to Elvis since
he died for our songs.
And when a friend said
I have a big appetite
I told him he should see
how cancer eats.

In the bakery across
the street there are loaves
of bread lying in a pile
in the window like baseball
bats. Today I bought one
then headed to the park
to hit a few balls out
or get into a game.

By the time I got there
I had eaten most
of the loaf, until it fit
in my hand like a club.
So I took it home to make
a sandwich, knowing

this way I'll never get
to first base.

The truth is I like to travel.
Last month I met a woman
with a small birthmark
on her thigh that's shaped
like France. How easy it is
to go there now, if only
to touch Paris with my tongue.

Learning to Pray

Before I was ten
the priest who kept
his eyes in bags changed
wine into blood every Mass
but I only tasted
the Gallo my mother
let me sip from her glass.
When his sermons shook
pews and scared angels
on the walls until they flapped
their stone and flew away,
I just stared through the beard
of a saint who was stained
in paint on the church windows.

My parents took me
to a small white chapel
every summer near the shore
that sat like a gull I knew
would never fly. Every time
my father leaned over
and told me to think God
my fingers went stiff,
my head bent with prayer
and halo until I'd look
out the window, past
the parking lot whose cars

were giant and fin, to the fields
that went on corn for miles.
I let my legs turn into stalks,
believed my soul was starch.

One August night we stayed in
the basement safe from a storm
that knocked Fairfield on its side
and any tree that wasn't
oak enough to take it.
When wind shook the house
like Elvis, my mother
told me to close my eyes
and pray. Instead I watched
the walls minuet with candlelight
and thought of the girl
next door who smelled like flowers.

Dogs

My brother and his wife
bought a hunting dog.
It's white with black patches.
There's one that's shaped
like Rhode Island, a small state
that isn't too heavy for a three-
month-old puppy to carry
around on his back. As
he gets older, stronger and puts
on weight, it will stretch
into Texas.

They have already taught
him to sit but he is still
too young to learn about Jesus,
so when they took him
to the beach, he tried walking
on water, fell in then turned
and attacked a wave,
ripping it to shreds.

A mound of cookie dough
on a plate is how he sleeps
on a round mattress and
dreams of rabbits or grouse.
For now a tennis ball
is enough to hunt down,

and sheets flying like ghosts
over rose bushes from
a neighbor's clothesline
is what makes him bark.

My brother and I take him
out on the lawn, throw
him a stick into tall grass.
He runs after it, his ears
that will never be trained
bounce and flap like a loose
shirt. He comes back
with the stick in his mouth
and every dog we ever
had as kids following him.
We can't believe how many
years have gone by since
we've seen them. Then we sit
down on the grass, smile
and watch all our dogs
running.

Born Again

Things are working out
on this job now that I'm
learning how to hold on
to a broom the way I should
have held on to my wife.
I prefer jobs where I can make
things with my hands
but last week I was grateful
to make the rent.

At least this job has benefits:
all the cigarette butts I sweep
up that are worth smoking
are mine. Before taking a break,
I find one, smooth it out,
light up, then walk over
to the window, holding the broom
like a rifle since I'm about
to kill ten minutes.

As I look around at the tenements
that shake from the subways
or from the cold, I realize
this kind of neighborhood is for
people like me in order to dream
as soon as we figure out
rainbows are never over the river

after rain but in oil stains
on the street where cars were parked
or stolen.

Behind the playground where some
guys come in warm weather
to shoot baskets, others to shoot up,
I see the building where I found
Jesus again gazing down from
the large mural on its side.
He looked Latin so I began
praying in Spanish and even
though He keeps fading, I
keep believing. Today for instance,
as I passed Him on my way
to work I pretended not to notice
how He now holds a cross
in His brick.

The Corner Where Jimmy Cagney Learned How to Act Tough

I moved out of my parents'
home and into my first
apartment on 78th Street.
It was the top floor of a five-
flight walk-up and at least
three floors higher than any rent
I could afford.

I was young, thought I was
pretty hot and brought girls up
before realizing it was
the apartment that made
them melt, not me.

The used air conditioner I bought
from the guy downstairs
wasn't any cooler than he was
and did little to help.
I even tried hanging posters
around of Steve McQueen,
Mick Jagger, James Dean
but found out although
they were hip they weren't cool.

The old woman living next
to me with her cat she called Dog

advised me to store away
a few days of every heat wave
then bring them out in winter
since the furnace keeps
breaking down. She said,
"August feels great in December."

She was right. On a few
mornings the radiator
hissed at me as if I were
a bad guy and the pipes
kept banging like the girl
across the street who kept
her bedroom blinds up.
Most days there was no heat.

She also told me that Jimmy
Cagney grew up around
the block on 77th, went
to the grammar school on York
and got his tough guy stance
in the movies from a pimp
who stood all day in front
of the building on the corner
of 78th and 1st.

The next day I went to look
at the building. Although
the pimp hadn't been there

for over sixty years, a deli
was, so anyone could
go in and buy a sandwich
just to prove on that corner
the roast beef was still
as tough as it gets.

Apple Spider

My niece at age four
is already tired
of the language as we
know it. Instead
of orange juice she asked
for a glass of apple
spider and at lunch
at a diner in town
she wanted me to put
a quarter in the little
juice box next
to the table and play
a song.

When we got home
I walked up into her
bedroom in search
of some sort of proof
that she is what I always
suspected: a genius.
Perhaps there would be
books on linguistics,
philosophy, Shakespeare
or essays by Pound
who might have ignited
her passion to "make it new."

But there was nothing
by Plato under her purple
hippo, no critical works
amongst her coloring
books or Socrates hidden
behind her dolls. Later
when her mother claimed
her daughter can't even
read and the classics
for a four-year-old
are Barney and Lamb Chop,
I still wasn't convinced.

So when my niece
told me she heard
I liked poet trees,
then asked where do
they grow, we both
picked up our cold
glasses of root beard
held on to each other's
hand, then headed out
the door to see if any
were growing in
the backyard.

Taxi Ride

I hop into a cab
and when the driver says
where to, I check to see
which way the heavy traffic
is going then tell him
to follow it downtown.

He cuts through Central Park
the way I should have cut
through the crap that day
and didn't. I rest my head
against the seat that is as soft
as a woman's chest and think
for the first time in my life
I might be able to fall
in love with vinyl.

When I was a kid
I had an uncle whose round
face would light up
with a smile after a few drinks,
mess up my hair then give
me whatever change he had.
That's what the moon
looks like tonight, an uncle
working on another drink
and ready to put his hand

in his pocket to fork over
a couple of bucks.

Apartment lights gleaming
from high-rises around the Park
are mixed in with stars
that slid down from the sky
during the heat wave last
week. Its hard to tell them
apart. At least I know in
this part of the city any star
I can reach by elevator
isn't worth the ride.

We come out on 58th Street.
Broadway glitters like a bracelet
filled with jewels and waiting
to be bought. I figure
it's a good idea to come back
for it later, then give it
to a woman who'll appreciate
how these lights sparkle
in all kinds of weather
and why traffic is the rarest
of gems whenever it dangles
from your wrist.

III. Amalfi Coast

First Day on the Amalfi Coast

When we first reached
the Amalfi coast
we pulled the car over
to stare at mountains
that peaked at one thousand feet
but didn't grow tired
and moved south towards
Salerno under sky
so clear I knew it would
have answers to any
questions we packed
and got past customs.

The Tyrrhenian sea was clean
as any joke my mother told
and the tiny white boats
anchored in front of a beach
were a piece of paper
someone tore up and threw
off a bluff. Below us
Positano stood up,
built into rock, home
on top of home that will
never lie down like the towns
I lived in back home.

In the distance
the large white sheet

covering a mountain's foot
is Priano where we
are going to spend the first
few nights if it doesn't
blow off rock next wind.

Before we get back into
the car, I look around
once more, knowing I can
comprehend rock, sky
and water but little Italian.
At least by the time
the voices on the beach
below reach me, they
translate into English.
Perhaps even here, if
I can keep some distance
I'll be able to understand
everything.

Grilled Fish

We had lunch
in a local trattoria
built into coastal rock,
picked a table on the deck
a few feet above water
that looked like the last
good novel I dove into.

A waiter came over
leaning on two metal canes.
He walked like stone
and his English was a coastline
of jagged rock. His smile
brought the sun closer,
suggested local specials,
and we said *grazie*
to things the sea didn't
need that day.

Another waiter brought
a pitcher of wine
with a round gold peach,
a tiny moon you can peel,
resting on the bottom.
We drank it with a salad
and tomatoes so sweet
and red the church should

make Satan blue.

Our main dish was grilled
fish who hadn't lost
their heads to the chef's knife,
or over the wrong women
the way I did a while back.
We didn't recognize them
either. They might have been
French, swam down here
for the day, then were tricked
by hook or net.

They tasted as rich
as the sun resting
on waves filled
with every gold coin
from every ship that sank
since Caesar and kept
rolling towards shore.

Swimming

I'd like to attend
the schools these small
fish swim in to learn
how this water stays
so clear and if it's envy
of sky and rock that turns
it green. Lack of wind
or therapy must calm
waves and extra salt
helps me float.

On my back, I look up
at mountains holding
homes in their cliffs.
Some sit so high
at night with their lights
on, they mix with stars.
And if I were a local,
I would have known better
than to pick a kitchen
light to make a wish.

The current takes me out
even though there is no
sail on my chest, and where
I can see a twelfth-century
tower that was built to warn

of Saracen invaders
who scared towns into
mountains, and when they
couldn't find God in churches,
killed priests instead.
Tourists are the only invaders
today along with tide
and boats from Capri.

By now I'm wet
enough to understand
the Tyrrhenian sea must love
this coastline to be so warm
and maybe even me,
on my back, with the sun
on my lips, floating.

The Ride to Amalfi

The road to Amalfi
winds along cliffs
that are narrow as any
thought my uncle ever had.
I look out at the sky that goes
on and on like two locals
talking and see a fish flying
north towards Naples,
its scales gleaming in the sun.
When it is over a yacht
that could fit in my niece's
bathtub, it becomes a jet.

I close my eyes when
we come to a turn and try
not to look down over the ledge
where the drop is deeper
than the debt it took me years
to climb out of. The bus driver
tells us everyone who lives here
believes the rock up ahead
looks like the Madonna. I try
to think of a prayer with stone
in it, then a quick blessing,
with a pebble or two but can't
as it becomes just another
opportunity that passes me by.

On a ridge above us, there must
be enough soil for an orchard—
trees, two by two, in long lines
like young soldiers, fresh troops
still green behind the leaves
marching off to harvest, armed
with branches and lemons hanging
like grenades from their shoulders.
Then around the next turn
and at the bottom of the road,
the harbor and town open up
the way a man clearing his conscience
does, with the sun staring down
and listening like a priest who forgives
absolutely nothing.

The Last Saint

Even too much wine
can't stop all the hurt
you packed, but thought
Customs would never let
you bring into the country.
When they asked if you
had anything to declare,
you said the last ten years.

Somehow you can still
walk past the medieval
tower that tonight is just
how the Amalfi coastline
gets a hard-on for water,
cars, moon or anything
that moves. So you sit
on a bench.

Low tide rubbing against
rock is how a song finds
a way out of your throat.
And to think you couldn't
speak a word of Italian
when the night began.
But since English never

made any sense and makes
even less now, you decide
never to speak it again.

A couple is standing in
front of you. The man looks
Polish enough to be the pope
and the woman with him
is so large they must rub
her thighs down with olive oil
to squeeze her into Rome.
They are laughing but since
it's a joke you know the punch
line to, you laugh even louder.

Then they are gone and there
is a church like the one
in Sorrento where Christ
is stone. Before you think
about converting to concrete,
you are in an alley leaning
against a building older
than Octavian. A woman
is kneeling in front of you
opening your belt. And
this is where it happens,
the very moment when
you become the last saint
on the face of the earth
who doesn't have a prayer.

St. Andrew's Head

In the tenth century A.D.
St. Andrew preached
his way down the southern
coast of Italy. Somewhere
between Sorrento and
Positano, he decided he must
leave something he valued
most to the Church when he
died. You might have thought:
a pouch of pepper, a few
drachmas, a favorite pair
of sandals repaired new
in Priano or even the goat
he converted by mistake,
when it was tied to a nearby
tree listening as he preached
to a group of Salerno pagans.
Instead St. Andrew decided
to leave the one true
and holy apostolic Church
his most prized possession—
his head. The same head
that now rests in a glass
box in the Dumo Cathedral
in the town of Amalfi.

The summer I visited
Amalfi, July was the hottest
on record before melting it.
Even the the Tyrrhenian Sea
looked more damp then wet.
Cafés surrounding the piazza
sold espresso dark
as midnight if you don't
pour in milk, stars or moon.
But I kept drinking water
from a woman's breast
who had been squirting it
from a fountain, and into
the mouths of locals and tourists
for centuries. Most
of the town goes back
to the Middle Ages, the sun
all the way back to Caesar.
I don't recall if the heat
caused the sun to slide down
the sky that looked more Spanish
than Italian or if a mountain
grew and covered it,
but by 4 P.M. half of the piazza
was cut in shade darker
than wine, and cool enough
for me to head up
the cathedral steps.

A few locals were sitting
on them. A large man,
who could sink Capri,
smoked a cigarette on
the first step. A few above
him an old woman, with a face
lined like a river after
it lost its water to drought,
ate a sandwich. A step
above her a young boy
pointed to my chest and
said, *American*. The sweat
stain on my shirt had formed
a map of the U.S. I took
it off and kept my T-shirt on,
making it easier to climb
the rest of the steps with all
fifty states flung over
my shoulder. I headed
inside; just another tourist
there to look in the face
of a man who's had nothing
to hold onto for centuries,
the head of a saint in a glass box,
his eyes closed to the world.

IV. Leaning Against August

Two Nickels

You walk past the old
arthritic woman who sits
by her window and waves
as you pass. On good days
she rocks back to Poland.

Jimmy "The Vet" stands on
the corner with a Greek
paper coffee cup. He's wearing
an army coat left over
from the wrong war and warns
you about the Cong along 3rd.
You thank him, promise to keep
your head down, then drop
fifty cents into the roof of the Parthenon
he holds in his hand.

If O.T.B. were open,
you'd place a bet on the bump
in the middle of 2nd Street.
Every time the No. 6 bus hits it,
you'd get paid off in all
the rattling fenders you need.

You stop in the topless bar
on 4th that feels colder

inside than it is outside.
The owner keeps costs
down by letting the girls
shake the heat up when they come
on at eight.

You order a draft
since the drinks are too
watered down to warm anything.
When the first girl comes on,
her legs look longer
than any unemployment line
you've ever been on and has a body
that knows how to talk.
It gets through to you the way
your first wife never could.
The next girl to come on
looks familiar. You realize
she danced here last week
as a blonde. Tonight she makes
you see red, but nothing
can change the good mood
you're in.

When you walk out after
midnight, the city begins
to sway and snow starts
falling. It's the color of the head
on the last beer you had,
and when a flake lands on

your lips, it makes you thirsty
all over again.

Before you can begin
walking home, an old drunk
comes over, asks if you
can spare any change
and begins telling you
that he once had the hottest
act on Broadway.
You smile, search your pockets,
then hand him your last
two nickels for a comeback.

Flying South

Noon was early
and the flight to Atlanta
late, so we took off
on time. As the plane left
the runway, I watched
the Throg's Neck Bridge shrink
in price until it was a souvenir
I could buy with the change
in my pocket and pin
on my lapel.

The passenger next to me
introduced himself before I was able
to count how many quarters
I had. He was in stocks
and a good mood. When I asked
for a tip, he recommended
marriage then reached
for the kids he was sitting on.

He showed me every family
photo in his wallet
and if he hadn't left to visit
a friend in the back,
I wouldn't have noticed
our wings slice through a cloud.
Rain poured from its side

but at least helped end
the drought in Delaware.

Fasten Your Seat Belt signs
flashed every time we hit
turbulence or a prayer on its way up,
making me realize that living near
an airport had something to do
with mine never getting answered.
From now on would only pray
after making sure there was nothing
in flight.

A stewardess made her way down
the aisle, asked if I'd like
something to drink then poured
a scotch over Virginia.
I sipped it slowly, making it last
a few thousand miles
until the captain said we'd land
in twenty minutes.

I could make out farmland,
as we descended,
cut into squares then stitched
into a quilt to keep soil warm.
It was the color green
I had been looking for
but from where I sat, I decided
it was too small for my bed

back home. And then Atlanta
appeared, spread out like a newspaper
that I tried reading
before taking off my glasses
since I couldn't find a single article
on why I came.

Sand

I stop in a café and find
a table near the window.
A waitress with purple spikes
stuck in her head
places a cloudy glass of water
in front of me. It looks
like last Tuesday, so I gulp
it down then head to
the bathroom to make sure
I piss another day away.

As I walk back to my table,
I notice it has begun
to flurry but the snow isn't
as white as it should be,
looking like more leftovers
from the last storm. And
perhaps it's the way my head
kept spinning over a woman
who never had any time for me
even after I bought her a watch,
that made me concerned
for the car in the parking space
across the street whose tire kept
spinning on a patch of ice.

By the time the waitress

brings over the coffee I ordered,
the driver opened the trunk
got out some sand, the color
of snow whenever it tans,
and threw it around the tire
giving it something to hold onto,
then got back in behind the wheel
and drove away.

I took a hit on the coffee,
and came up with a plan.
The next time my head starts
spinning over a woman I'm stuck
on this winter, I'll remember to stay
calm, be myself and just in case I need
something else to hold onto, keep
a little sand in my pocket.

Stems

When we were together
I always woke first
just to watch you sleep
then would kiss you
until dawn tangled
in your hair,
the sun curling
gently against your eyes.

I still don't know
where the end begins
between a man and a woman.
So I think of flowers
and how my arms
became stems
every time I reached
to touch your face—
the delicate bloom
of your smile.

If I could, I'd make
every day begin with your mouth,
and the night you gazed up
at me, your eyes glittered
with a constellation
I should have named after you
and made a wish,

since twilight will never
be that close again.

For the past month
I've climbed into bed and covered
myself with a blanket
of fog we trimmed from July
to help keep us warm,
but it never reaches
the warmth of your arm
lying across my chest.

When I finally fall asleep
I have the same dream:
snow begins falling
as you sit quietly before me
and let me cut your hair.

Lungs

York Avenue was under
construction. Tiny rocks
hitting the bottom of my car
sounded like my best
friend's lungs every time
he fought for one more breath.
I pulled over to the side
of the road and waited
the way I sat and waited
at the side of his bed,
got out of the car and walked
over to the East River.

I leaned against the railing
that offered the support
I didn't need but could use
and watched a tugboat turn
red, straining to pull
a huge barge uptown.
I tried to look over the head
of Queens but Roosevelt Island
wouldn't bend down
and became just something
else to get in my way.

Since it wasn't rush hour
the river flowed smoothly

and in the heat the water
looked a bit dryer than usual.
I couldn't help noticing
a factory smoking its four stacks
and wondered if there were
any tumors growing in
its furnace.

My friend said after he was
gone to look for him here.
It took a while until a cool
wind from the ocean reached
the river's mouth, helping
a sailboat slide down its
throat and the wings of a gull
gliding from its stern
like a kite is where I found him.

I watched the boat sail
under the Tram hanging
like a basket from wire
with a dozen eggs or
passengers visible from
its windows, then under
the 59th Street Bridge that kept
cars dry.

I kept watching until
the river curved like

a woman's hip and he was
gone again. I should
have known this is how
he'd do it and decided
as I walked back to the car,
he never looked better.

While You Are Away

—*for Celia*

I wanted to give you
something special tonight.
Perhaps dinner next
to the harbor where a warm
breeze comes in off
the ocean from Europe
and plucks the riggings
of sailboats along the docks
like Spanish guitars.
But it's winter, almost
midnight and you still
haven't arrived. You see
I've come to the realization
that everything that is broken
in me is yours. So I do
what I believe is right:
place two glasses on
the table near the window,
open a bottle of claret
and pour some into each,
then turn off the lights
wait and watch as the moon
floats in our wine.

Spine

Between 9th and 10th Streets
an old woman passes you
in a polka-dot outfit.
A few minutes later you look
up and see the moon
for the first time and wonder
if the wind blew off
one of the loose dots from her dress.
You consider climbing the eighty-
story apartment building
across the street to peel the moon
off the sky and give it back
to her but you've never aimed
for anything that high in your life
and decide now is not the time
to start. Instead you turn
around and make the building
your spine, since you always
had doubts about the one
you had, so when the next woman
you sleep with wants to slide
her hand up your back
she'll just have to wait
for the elevator if she really
wants her fingertips to reach
your skull.

Renting July

I rent July in a town
that once grew on whales.
Locals still think fish,
work water but this time
of year thank cod when their
nets are full.

Today I went to the beach
for the first time and
with the tide out the shore
line looked lean and
in great shape with its muscles
gleaming in the sun.

Sailboats moved like sharks
around a lighthouse
they scared white but it never
leaves, knowing it has to warn
ships about rock each fog.
I then spread my towel out,
lay down on Rhode Island,
rubbed oil on myself to help
a cloud slide across my chest
and closed my eyes.

When the woman I still love
came by, saying she wanted

me back and would never leave,
I knew something was wrong,
woke and sat up, I was already
red as a sore throat and decided
I'd had enough sun for the day.

As I got up, I noticed a string
of smoke in the sky a jet
left behind. Before it faded
I reached up took it and tied
any more thoughts I had of her
into a package I tucked under
my arm and carried home.

Kansas in My Lungs

As a kid, I just seemed
to know things. When
the nuns taught us about
saints and angels, it never
made any sense with
Christina Huxley sitting in
the desk next to mine.
I knew then she was
the closest I'd ever get
to heaven.

The day my dad brought
home a shepherd puppy,
he said it was German;
I didn't have the heart
to tell him it looked more
Italian around the eyes.

I was good in math class
but when things didn't
add up, I'd turn on my
parents' old TV and find
the correct answer since
everything was clear in
black and white.

When the parish priest came
into class once a week
to teach religion and talked
about the mystery of faith,
I knew the only mystery
worth solving was on the face
of every girl who made me
look down at my shoes and blush.

I'm still single; gave up
cigarettes a few months
ago. I just couldn't handle
the commitment, then
switched over to cigars
until my five-year-old
niece said if I kept smoking
I'd end up with Kansas
in my lungs.
That really scared me.
I had coughed up topsoil
before but there was no
way my lungs could deal
with all that farmland.
And I found there are some
things my niece knows too.
So the next day I decided
to quit smoking everything
for good.

Leaning Against August

Today the air is thick enough
for me to lean against
August and tie my shoe.
But no matter how hot this city
gets, I couldn't live anywhere else.
Even the garbage on the sidewalks
is really the only way to talk
trash and I can't deny anymore
there's something to the stain
a drunk pissed against
a building on 4th now that it
dried into a portrait of Christ.

Maybe I just go for how days
never dawn here—it's more
in the way they quietly show up.
Like the sun does when it looks
bloated and the color of beer
in this haze and hung over
2nd Avenue. Or any street that hums
with air conditioners resting
on windowsills like Polish
grandmothers looking down
at America when it was only
a few blocks long.

When my own a.c. broke down
I found it cheaper to play
my Miles Davis collection since
it cools off the entire apartment.
And I found it's a good idea
to keep extra change in my pockets
in case I see the blind man
who stands between 3rd and 4th
holding a paper cup with his dog
sleeping like a bagel at his feet.

He stands a block away
from where the woman
I've been seeing lives.
She's been unemployed for a year
but to keep busy she works
hard on our relationship.
I really care for her but until
I feel more, I keep stopping
in the little Italian joint across
the street from her place for a slice
of the pizza I love.

I guess the point is I can
adapt. I did to these buildings
the city rubbed against
so many times they turned dark.
Most are old tenements
no more than five stories

that I've read so many times
I can even quote you a couple
of floors by heart.

KEVIN PILKINGTON is a member of the writing faculty at Sarah Lawrence College and teaches in the graduate program at Manhattanville College. He is the author of four collections: his last chapbook won the Ledge Poetry Prize and his collection *Spare Change* was the La Jolla Poets Press National Book Award winner. His work has appeared in many anthologies including *Birthday Poems: A Celebration*, *Western Wind*, and *Contemporary Poetry of New England*. He has been nominated for three Pushcart Prizes and his poems have appeared in numerous magazines including: *Poetry, Ploughshares, Iowa Review, Boston Review, Yankee, Hayden's Ferry, Columbia, Greensboro Review, The Louisville Review, Gulf Coast, Confrontation*.